1628
This edition reprinted in 1992 by Tiger Books International PLC, London
© 1987 Coombe Books
Printed and bound in Singapore
ISBN 1 85501 111 5

Text by
Beverley Piper
Photography by
Peter Barry
Designed by
Philip Clucas

COCKTAILS
AND
SNACKS

TIGER BOOKS INTERNATIONAL
LONDON

Contents

Avocado Cheese Balls (top), Celery Boats (above) and Prawn Stuffed Eggs (right).

Snacks

Avocado Cheese Balls

PREPARATION TIME: 30 minutes + 30 minutes to refrigerate

MAKES: 25 party snacks

1 medium size, ripe avocado
15-30ml (1-2 tblsp) single cream or
    yoghurt
1 clove garlic, crushed (optional)
5ml (1 tsp) lemon juice
75g (3oz) finely grated low fat
    Cheddar cheese
5ml (1 tsp) made mustard
25g (1oz) fresh breadcrumbs
½ small onion, finely chopped
Freshly ground black pepper to taste
30ml (2 tblsp) freshly chopped parsley
50g (2oz) toasted almond nibs

Halve the avocado and twist apart.
Remove stone. Peel each half.
Mash the avocado flesh in a
medium size mixing bowl. Add
the cream or yoghurt, crushed
garlic, lemon juice, grated cheese,
mustard, breadcrumbs, onion and
seasoning, mixing with a fork until
a stiff paste results.
Using cold, damp hands, roll
rounded teaspoons of the mixture
into balls. Roll half in the finely
chopped parsley to coat. Roll
remaining balls in the cold, toasted
nuts to coat.
Refrigerate for 30 minutes before
serving.

Prawn Stuffed Eggs

PREPARATION TIME: 15 minutes

MAKES: 12 party snacks

6 eggs, size 4
50g (2oz) vegetable margarine or low
    fat spread
1 clove garlic, crushed
75g (3oz) cooked, peeled prawns,
    chopped
2.5ml (½ tsp) finely chopped basil
Freshley ground black pepper to taste
Low fat milk if necessary

Garnish:
Tiny pieces of red pepper
Bed of lettuce

Hard boil the eggs, stirring as they
come to the boil. Drain and plunge
immediately into cold water.
Allow to cool completely. Shell
and cut each egg in half

lengthwise. Remove yolks. Set
aside.
Cream the margarine or low fat
spread with the crushed clove of
garlic. Beat in the egg yolks,
prawns, basil and black pepper to
taste. Add a little milk if
necessary until a soft consistency
results.
Fill the egg whites with the
prepared mixtures. Serve
garnished with a tiny piece of red
pepper.
Note: This snack may be prepared
in the morning provided it is kept
airtight in the refrigerator until just
before serving.

Celery Boats

PREPARATION TIME: 15-20 minutes

MAKES: 100 party snacks

2 heads celery, cleaned

For the Fish Paté:
2 medium size smoked mackerel
    fillets with peppercorns
100g (4oz) smoked salmon, chopped
Juice ½ lemon
100g (4oz) curd cheese
5ml (1 tsp) tomato purée
5ml (1 tsp) creamed horseradish
45ml (3 tblsp) thick-set natural
    yoghurt
1 tblsp fresh parsley sprigs

Garnish:
Sprigs of fresh mint
Lumpfish caviar

Make the paté. Skin the mackerel
and flake the fish into the bowl of a
food processor, using the metal
blade, or into a liquidiser goblet.
Process to chop finely – 5-7
seconds. Add the roughly chopped
smoked salmon, the lemon juice,
curd cheese, tomato purée,
creamed horseradish, yoghurt,
fresh parsley sprigs and seasoning.
Process until smooth.
Cut the celery into boats and pipe
or spread with the paté.
Garnish with the lumpfish caviar
and sprigs of mint. Serve cold.
Note: This snack may be prepared
in the morning provided it is kept
airtight in the refrigerator until
ready to serve.

Savoury Eclairs

PREPARATION TIME: 20-30 minutes

COOKING TIME: 20 minutes

MAKES: 15 party snacks

1 recipe choux pastry (see recipe for
    Cheese Aigrettes)
Beaten egg to glaze
Salt and freshly ground black pepper
    to taste
175g (6oz) cream cheese, at room
    temperature
5ml (1 tsp) tomato puree
15ml (1 tblsp) chopped chives
100g (4oz) lean cooked ham,
    chopped
25-50g (1-2oz) almond nibs

To Garnish:
Finely chopped fresh parsley.

Make the choux pastry exactly as
directed for Cheese Aigrettes, but
do not add the grated cheese.
Season. Allow to cool.
Using a large piping bag and a
1cm (½ in) plain tube, pipe fingers
of the choux paste about 2.5cm
(1 in) long onto a greased baking
sheet. Brush all over with the
beaten egg. Sprinkle with the
almond nibs. Bake on the top
shelf of a pre-heated oven 200°C,
400°F, Gas Mark 6, for about 20
minutes, or until puffed up and
golden.
Transfer to a cooling tray and
immediately make a slit in the side
of each with a sharp vegetable
knife. This will allow the steam to
escape. Allow to cool.
For the filling. Beat together the
cream cheese, cream and tomato
puree. Fold in the chives and ham.
Season to taste.
Using a large piping bag fitted
with 1cm (½ in) plain tube, or a
teaspoon, fill the eclairs with the
cream cheese mixture.
Serve immediately, sprinkled with
the chopped parsley.
Note: The eclairs may be baked in
the morning and left on the
cooling tray until ready to fill.

Cheese Straws

PREPARATION TIME: 20-30 minutes

COOKING TIME: 15-20 minutes

MAKES: 18-20 party snacks

200g (8oz) plain flour
5ml (1 tsp) mustard powder
Salt and freshly ground black pepper
  to taste
Pinch of cayenne pepper
100g (4oz) butter
100g (4oz) mature Cheddar cheese,
  finely grated
1 egg yolk
Cold water to mix   mixed with
A little beaten egg

Sieve the flour, mustard powder, seasoning and cayenne pepper. Rub in the butter. Fork in the cheese. Mix to a stiff dough with the egg yolk and water.

Roll the pastry out to a thickness of 1 cm (½ in). Cut into straws about 10 cm (4 in) long. Cut out a pastry ring, using two plain cutters. Brush ring and straws with beaten egg.

Arrange on baking sheet and bake just above centre of a preheated oven 200°C, 400°F, Gas Mark 6, for 15-20 minutes, or until golden. Serve the cooled straws, stacked in the ring.

Smoked Salmon Flowers (right) Savoury Eclairs (centre right) and Cheese Straws (far right).

Smoked Salmon Flowers

PREPARATION TIME: 20-30 minutes

MAKES: 12 party snacks

175g (6oz) plain flour
75g (3oz) butter or margarine
2.5ml (½ tsp) salt
Cold water to bind
2 eggs, size 2
30ml (2 tblsp) milk
25g (1oz) butter
Salt and freshly ground black pepper
   to taste
15ml (1 tblsp) double cream
100g (4oz) thin slices smoked salmon

To Garnish:
A few chopped chives.

Make the patties. Sieve flour and salt. Rub in margarine. Mix to a firm dough with the water. Roll out and cut 12 rounds using a fluted cutter. Line 12 jam tart tins. Prick with a fork.

Bake blind on the second shelf of a pre-heated oven 200°C, 400°F, Gas Mark 6, for 10-15 minutes. Remove from tins and allow to cool.

Beat eggs and milk together, and season lightly. Melt butter in medium pan over low heat. Stir in egg mixture and cook over a low heat, stirring all the time until mixture scrambles. Remove from heat and allow to cool slightly, stirring. Stir in cream. Set aside to cool.

Cut smoked salmon into strips and line each pastry case. Top with a little of the cooled scrambled egg and garnish each salmon flower with a few chopped chives.

Parmesan New Potatoes (top),
Bacon Mushrooms (above
right) and Spiced Nuts (right).

Parmesan New Potatoes

PREPARATION TIME: 10-15 minutes

COOKING TIME: about 10-18 minutes (depending on model)

MAKES: 15-16 party snacks

450g (1lb) tiny new potatoes, peeled, if required
50g (2oz) butter
2.5ml (½ tsp) salt (optional)
Grated Parmesan cheese
Finely chopped parsley

Put the potatoes into a roasta-bag. Dissolve the salt, if used, in 30ml (2 tblsp) cold water and add to the bag. Seal the bag loosely with a rubber band and place in a casserole dish.
Microwave on 100% (high) for
    7 minutes (700W oven)
    8-9 minutes (600W oven)
    10-12 minutes (500W oven)
In each case, turn the bag over once, half-way through cooking time. Set aside for 10 minutes.
Put the butter in a large mixing bowl and microwave on defrost for
    2-3 minutes (700W oven)
    3-4 minutes (600W oven)
    4-5 minutes (500W oven)
or until melted.
Drain the potatoes and toss in the melted butter. Sprinkle with parsley or Parmesan and serve hot or cold on cocktail sticks.

Bacon Mushrooms

PREPARATION TIME: 20-30 minutes

COOKING TIME: about 5-10 minutes (depending on model)

MAKES: 24 party snacks

12 rashers streaky bacon, de-rinded
24 small button mushrooms
50g (2oz) fine liver pate
Wooden cocktail sticks

To Serve:
1 whole grapefruit
Cocktail sticks

Using the back of a knife, stretch each rasher of bacon out on a chopping board.
Arrange 6 of the bacon slices on a microwave rack or on 2 sheets absorbent paper on a dinner plate. Cover with 2 sheets absorbent kitchen paper. Microwave on 100% (high) for
    2-3 minutes (700W oven)
    4-5 minutes (600W oven)
    5-7 minutes (500W oven)
Wipe the mushrooms clean and remove stalks. Stuff each

mushroom with a little liver pate. Cut each slice of partly cooked bacon in half, lengthways, and wrap each half around a stuffed mushroom. Secure with cocktail stick.
Arrange in a ring on the same dinner plate or roasting rack, standing on 2 clean sheets absorbent kitchen paper if using the dinner plate. Do not cover. Microwave on 100% (high) for about
    3 minutes (700W oven)
    4-4½ minutes (600W oven)
    5-6 minutes (500W oven)
Repeat with remaining bacon rolls. Serve on cocktail sticks, pushed into the grapefruit.
Note: This snack is best served within two hours of preparation.

Spiced Nuts

PREPARATION TIME: 10 minutes

COOKING TIME: about 7-12 minutes (depending on model)

MAKES: 350g (12oz) spiced nuts

100g (4oz) shelled, husked peanuts
100g (4oz) shelled, blanched almonds
100g (4oz) shelled, husked cashew nuts
15ml (1 tblsp) corn oil
15g (½oz) butter
2.5ml (½ tsp) ground ginger
2.5ml (½ tsp) ground cinnamon
2.5ml (½ tsp) cayenne pepper
Salt to taste

In a mixing bowl, combine the nuts.
Put the oil and butter in a 25cm (10 in) flan dish and microwave on 100% (high) for 1-2½ minutes or until the butter melts.
Sprinkle the spices over the nuts (do not add salt at this stage). Pour on the butter and oil and toss to coat.
Transfer the nuts to the flan dish and microwave uncovered on 100% (high) for about
    7-9 minutes (700W oven)
    10-12 minutes (600W oven)
    12-14 minutes (500W oven)
In all cases stir the nuts 2 or 3 times during the cooking time and remove when lightly golden as they will continue to colour when removed from the microwave.
Allow to stand for 5 minutes. Sprinkle with salt before serving hot or cold.
Note: When quite cold these nuts will keep well in an airtight container.

Sausage Toasties

PREPARATION TIME: 15-20 minutes

COOKING TIME: 20-30 minutes

MAKES: 24 party snacks

12 pork sausages, pricked
12 medium slices from a cut loaf
75g (3oz) butter
10ml (2 tsp) made mustard

Cut the crusts off the bread and roll each slice out flat with a rolling pin.
Stirring continuously, melt the butter and mustard together over a low heat. Brush each slice of bread with the melted mustard butter.
Roll each piece of prepared bread round a sausage to enclose completely. Cut in half to give 24 rolls.
Arrange on a baking sheet, join-side down, and bake on the second shelf of a pre-heated oven 170°C, 375°F, Gas Mark 5, for 20-30 minutes, until golden brown.
Serve hot or cold.

Stuffed Mushrooms

PREPARATION TIME: 20 minutes

COOKING TIME: 20 minutes

MAKES: 28 party snacks

60ml (4 tblsp) blue cheese
    mayonnaise
50g (2oz) cooked bacon, chopped
1 clove garlic, crushed
25g (1oz) fresh breadcrumbs
350g (12oz) button mushrooms,
    stalks removed
50g (2oz) butter

To Serve:
Croutons of toast.

Put the mayonnaise into a mixing bowl. Fold in the bacon, garlic and the breadcrumbs.
Melt the butter in a 25cm (10 in) flan dish in an oven preheated to 175°C, 350°F, Gas Mark 4. This will take about 7-10 minutes.
Fill the mushrooms, dark, gill side up, with the blue cheese mixture. Arrange in the hot butter. Using a pastry brush, carefully brush the butter round sides of each stuffed mushroom.
Bake, uncovered, for 10-15 minutes, then increase temperature to 190°C, 400°F, Gas Mark 6, for 5 minutes.
Serve, hot or cold, on the circles of toasted bread.

Asparagus Peanut Rolls

PREPARATION TIME: 20 minutes

MAKES: 14 party snacks

1 large brown loaf, uncut
50g (2oz) butter, at room temperature
10ml (2 tsp) smooth peanut butter
Few drops lemon juice
340g (12oz) can asparagus spears,
    drained

Garnish:
Lemon butterflies
Chicory leaves

Cut the crusts off the loaf.
Beat the peanut butter and lemon juice into the butter. Cut the bread thinly and roll each slice out flat with a rolling pin. Spread the bread with the flavoured butter and place a piece of drained asparagus on each piece of bread. Roll bread round asparagus to enclose completely. Trim asparagus stem if necessary.
Serve garnished with the lemon butterflies and chicory leaves.

Salami Open Sandwiches

PREPARATION TIME: 20 minutes

MAKES: 6 party snacks

6 slices rye bread
75g (3oz) cream cheese
18 slices of salami
A few drained asparagus tips
1 small onion, ringed
Slices of cucumber
1 Iceberg lettuce, shredded

Remove crusts and cut each slice of bread into an attractive shape. Spread thickly with cream cheese. Top with salami and decorate as required – see picture. Serve on a bed of Iceberg lettuce.
Note: It will be necessary to use a knife and fork for this snack.

Asparagus Peanut Rolls (left), Stuffed Mushrooms (below left) and Sausage Toasties (bottom).

Cauliflower and Courgette Fritters

PREPARATION TIME: 30 minutes
COOKING TIME: 20-30 minutes
MAKES: 45 party snacks

175g (6oz) cauliflower florets
175g (6oz) baby courgettes

For the Fritter Batter:
150g (5oz) self-raising flour
2.5ml (½ tsp) salt
1 egg
135ml (5 fl oz) cold water

Top and tail the courgettes and cut into bite size pieces. Do not wash either the courgettes or cauliflower florets but wipe clean with a damp cloth if necessary.
Make the batter. Sieve the flour and salt into a mixing bowl. Make a well in the centre. Separate the egg, putting the yolk into the well in the flour and the white into a clean, medium-sized mixing bowl. Adding the water gradually, mix the flour and egg yolk to a smooth batter with a wooden spoon. Whisk the egg white until standing in soft peaks and fold into the batter with a metal spoon.
Meanwhile, heat the oil in a deep fat fryer to 190°C (375°F). Dip the prepared vegetables into the batter to coat and then, using a slotted spoon, lower each piece of battered vegetable into the hot oil. Fry until crisp and golden.
Do not try to fry more than 8 pieces of vegetable at a time so that the temperature of the oil is maintained.
Drain on absorbent kitchen paper and serve piping hot accompanied by Seafood Dip (see recipe).

Cheese Aigrettes

PREPARATION TIME: 20-30 minutes
COOKING TIME: 30 minutes
MAKES: 25-27 party snacks

For the Choux Pastry:
150ml (¼ pint) cold water
50g (2oz) butter
65g (2½oz) plain flour
Salt and freshly ground pepper to taste
2 eggs, size 3, beaten

75g (3oz) grated Cheddar cheese
5ml (1 tsp) made mustard
Pinch cayenne pepper
Oil to deep fry

Put the water and butter into a medium saucepan. Bring the water to the boil. Stir to ensure butter has melted.
Turn off heat and immediately add the sifted flour and seasoning, all at once. Beat well with a wooden spoon until a ball of shiny dough results which leaves the side of the pan clean. Set aside for 5-10 minutes to cool slightly.
Gradually beat in the beaten eggs, a little at a time, until a thick, glossy paste results. Beat cheese, mustard and cayenne pepper into prepared choux pastry.
Meanwhile, heat the oil in a deep fat fryer to 190°C (375°F).
Fry teaspoons of the mixture in the deep fat until puffed up and golden brown. Do not fry more than 8 teaspoons of choux paste at a time so that the temperature of the oil is maintained.
Drain on absorbent kitchen paper and serve immediately.

Breaded Scampi

PREPARATION TIME: 20 minutes
COOKING TIME: 20-30 minutes
MAKES: 30 party snacks

450g (1lb) peeled Dublin Bay prawns, defrosted if frozen
1 egg, beaten
125-150g (4-5oz) fresh brown breadcrumbs
Oil to deep fry

Garnish:
Lemon wedges and fresh sprigs parsley

As an Accompaniment:
Tartare sauce

Blot the prawns as dry as possible on plenty of absorbent kitchen paper. This is particularly important if frozen prawns are used.
Put the beaten egg into a cereal bowl, and the breadcrumbs onto a dinner plate. Dip the prawns into the beaten egg and then in the breadcrumbs to coat. Repeat until all the prawns have been coated.
Meanwhile, heat the oil in the deep fat fryer to 375°F (190°C) and fry the prepared scampi, no more than 10 at a time, so that the temperature of the oil is maintained, until golden brown (about 5 minutes).
Drain on absorbent kitchen paper and serve hot, garnished with the lemon and parsley. Pass a bowl of tartare sauce round separately.

Cheese Aigrettes (left), Cauliflower and
Courgette Fritters (below) and Breaded Scampi
(bottom).

Cocktail Sausage Rolls with Apple

PREPARATION TIME: 30 minutes

COOKING TIME: about 20 minutes

MAKES: 30 party snacks

350g (12oz) packet frozen puff pastry, defrosted
450g (1lb) pork sausage meat
1 eating apple 100g (4oz) peeled, cored and chopped
Salt and freshly ground black pepper to taste
Flour
1 beaten egg

Roll the pastry out to a thickness of about 5mm (¼ in) and cut into 2 strips about 10cm (4 in) wide. Work the apple and seasoning into the sausage meat. Shape into two long rolls to fit the pastry. Dust sausage meat lightly with seasoned flour and arrange on each strip of pastry.

Brush the edges of each strip of pastry with beaten egg. Fold the pastry over and seal.

Using the back of a knife, knock up and then flute the edges. Make two slits with a sharp vegetable knife on the top of each roll at 1cm (½ in) intervals to allow the steam to escape.

Brush all over with beaten egg and cut into 2.5cm (1 in) pieces. Arrange on a dampened baking sheet and bake just above centre in a pre-heated oven at 210°C, 450°F, Gas Mark 7, for about 20 minutes, or until golden brown. Best served warm.

Spiced Chilli Savouries (above), Cocktail Sausage Rolls with Apple (right) and Salami Open Sandwiches (far right).

Spiced Chilli Savouries

PREPARATION TIME: 20 minutes
COOKING TIME: 10 minutes
MAKES: 30 party snacks

300g (12oz) raw minced beef
50g (2oz) fresh brown breadcrumbs
1 small onion, finely chopped
10ml (2 tsp) finely chopped oregano
10ml (2 tsp) ground chilli powder
15ml (1 tblsp) tomato purée
10ml (2 tsp) made mustard
Salt and freshly ground pepper to taste

½ a beaten egg
Seasoned flour for coating
25-50g (1-2oz) garlic butter, melted

Put the beef into a large mixing bowl. Add the breadcrumbs, onion, oregano, chilli powder, tomato purée, mustard and the seasoning.
Mix well. Bind the mixture together with the beaten egg.
Roll teaspoons of the mixture into small meat balls. Toss in the seasoned flour to coat.

Brush with the melted garlic butter and grill under a medium heat, turning occasionally until evenly browned.
Serve on cocktail sticks, accompanied by the mixed seafood dip (see recipe).
Note: This snack may be served hot or cold, but is best served within 2 hours of preparation.

Chinese Melon (top), Stuffed Vine Leaves
(above) and Peach with Parma Ham (left).

Stuffed Vine Leaves

PREPARATION TIME: 20 minutes

COOKING TIME: 15 minutes

MAKES: 20-24 party snacks

225g (8oz) packet vine leaves
100g (4oz) cooked chicken meat,
　minced
100g (4oz) cooked lean lamb,
　minced
30ml (2 tblsp) cooked brown rice
2 spring onions, chopped
5ml (1 tsp) tarragon, finely chopped
30ml (2 tblsp) apple sauce
Salt and freshly ground black pepper
　to taste
30ml (2 tblsp) grape seed oil or corn
　oil
1 medium onion, chopped
30ml (2 tblsp) tomato puree
15ml (1 tblsp) dry white wine

Carefully dip the vine leaves into a pan of boiling water. Drain well on a clean tea towel.
Combine the minced chicken and lamb, the rice, spring onions, the tarragon and apple sauce. Mix well. Season.
Put a small amount of the filling in the centre of each drained vine leaf. Roll up.
Put the oil into a large, shallow frying pan. Heat for 1-2 minutes, then fry the onion until soft but not brown. Stir in the tomato puree and wine. Season.
Stir in 30ml (2 tblsp) water. Lower the stuffed vine leaves carefully into the pan using a slotted spoon. Cover with a lid and simmer gently for 15 minutes, checking after 5 minutes that there is sufficient liquid.
Note: It will be necessary to use a knife and fork with this dish, which is delicious hot or cold.

Peach with Parma Ham

PREPARATION TIME: 20 minutes

MAKES: about 45 party snacks

2 large, ripe peaches
100g (4oz) Parma ham
Cocktail sticks

Peel the peaches – this is much easier if the peaches are covered with boiling water for 1-2 minutes first.
Halve the peeled peaches and remove the stone. Cut each half into bite size pieces.

Cut the ham into thin strips and roll one strip round each peach piece. Secure with cocktail sticks. Serve chilled.
Note: When fresh peaches are not available, use drained, canned pineapple pieces or cubes of fresh melon.

Chinese Melon

PREPARATION TIME: 40 minutes

COOKING TIME: 10 minutes

SERVES: 8-10 people

350g (12oz) fillet of pork, cut into
　2.5cm (1 in) cubes
1 green or yellow melon, chilled
Oil for brushing
Salt and freshly ground black pepper
　to taste
425g (15oz) can pineapple pieces in
　natural juice, drained and juice
　reserved

For the Optional Dressing:
5ml (1 tsp) soya sauce
30ml (2 tblsp) pineapple juice
1 clove garlic, crushed
Pinch ground ginger
15ml (1 tblsp) white wine vinegar
30ml (2 tblsp) olive oil

Brush the cubes of pork with a little oil. Season and thread onto kebab sticks or meat skewers. Grill under a medium grill, turning occasionally until well cooked. Set aside to cool.
Carefully cut the melon in half, horizontally. Remove seeds and discard. Remove melon flesh and dice. Serrate the melon shells.
Fill the serrated melon shells with the cooked pork cut into small pieces, the diced melon flesh and the pineapple pieces.
Put all the ingredients for the dressing into a screw-top jar. Screw on the lid. Shake to mix. Arrange the filled melon on a serving dish and, just before serving, pour over the prepared dressing, if using. Serve immediately with cocktail sticks.

Fish Kebabs

PREPARATION TIME: 15 minutes

COOKING TIME: 10 minutes

MAKES: 6 party snacks

350g (12oz) boneless cod, cubed
225g (8oz) large, peeled prawns
225g (8oz) lamb's liver, cut into pieces
225g (8oz) can pineapple rings
  drained and cut into pieces
50g (2oz) butter
1 clove garlic, crushed
5ml (1 tsp) finely chopped fresh parsley
6 bridge rolls
Butter for spreading (optional)
6 metal meat skewers

Load each skewer with alternating pieces of the prepared food; that is, a cube of cod, a prawn, a piece of lamb's liver and a piece of pineapple until each skewer is full. Put the butter, garlic and parsley into a small pan and set over a low heat, stirring until the butter has melted.

Brush the kebabs all over with the garlic butter, and grill, turning occasionally, until well cooked. Split the bridge rolls and butter if required. Slip the food off the kebab sticks into the prepared rolls.

Serve immediately with a choice of relish.

Crab Rounds

PREPARATION TIME: 20 minutes

MAKES: 16 party snacks

2 cucumbers, ends removed
170g (6oz) can crab meat
95g (3½oz) can pink salmon, skin
  and bones removed
60ml (4 tblsp) double cream, whipped
5ml (1 tsp) tomato purée
5ml (1 tsp) lemon juice
Salt and freshly ground black pepper
  to taste

Garnish:
Slices of pimento olives
Parsley

Cut both the cucumbers evenly into 8 large rings. Using a teaspoon, hollow out a boat in each ring, leaving a shell 5mm (¼ in) thick. Sprinkle with salt and leave them to stand upside down while preparing filling.

In a mixing bowl combine the drained, chopped crab meat, the drained, flaked salmon, the cream, tomato purée, lemon juice and seasoning to taste. Rinse cucumber rings and blot dry. Fill each prepared cucumber boat with the crab mixture.

Garnish with a slice of pimento olive and a tiny piece of parsley before serving.

Note: If liked, the cucumber boats may be crimped as in the picture, before hollowing out. This is rather time-consuming, however.

Mixed Seafood Dip

PREPARATION TIME: 15 minutes

SERVES: 8 people

100g (4oz) large, cooked, peeled
  prawns
100g (4oz) smoked salmon
100g (4oz) lobster meat

For the Dip:
300ml (5fl oz) soured cream
75g (3oz) Stilton cheese, crumbled
15ml (1 tblsp) natural yoghurt
45ml (3 tblsp) mayonnaise
5ml (1 tsp) fresh basil, finely chopped
5ml (1 tsp) lemon juice
1-2 cloves garlic, crushed (optional)
Salt and freshly ground black pepper
  to taste

To Accompany:
Strips of peeled carrot
Strips of cucumber, peel left on

Prepare the dip. Put the soured cream into a mixing bowl. Stir in the Stilton, yoghurt, mayonnaise, basil, lemon juice, garlic if used, and seasoning to taste. Mix well. Transfer the dip to an attractive serving dish, set in the centre of a large plate.

Put the seafood in groups around the dish of dip, leaving the prawns whole, cutting the lobster meat into bite-sized pieces and making the smoked salmon into rolls, secured with cocktail sticks. Add the sticks of carrot and cucumber and serve immediately.

Note: This recipe may be prepared on the morning of the party but keep covered with cling film in the refrigerator until ready to serve.

Crab Rounds (right), Mixed Seafood
Dip (below) and Fish Kebabs (bottom).

Cocktails

FIRST WORDS

'Shaken or stirred?', a question dating back half a century to the days when every home entertainer possessed at least one cocktail shaker, and a very well-stocked bar. The last few years have witnessed the resurrection of the cocktail – along with all its associated paraphernalia. The revival has been accompanied by an enthusiastic interest in the composition of the concoctions themselves, and this book aims to provide the answers to the questions asked by anyone wishing to try their hand at cocktail-mixing.

YOU WILL NEED . . .

Most of the equipment used by the cocktail bartender can be improvised from basic kitchen tools. It is, however, worth investing in a simple stainless-steel *cocktail shaker* – although you can use a wide-mouthed fruit juice bottle with a screw-top lid. A *mixing glass* or a plain glass jug with a two pint capacity is needed to make any drink which requires stirring with ice. The stirrer is ideally a long-handled *barspoon*, and the drink, once chilled, is poured through a *cocktail or 'Hawthorne' strainer*. Any of the more exotic concoctions – particularly those made with fresh fruit – as well as drinks which incorporate eggs or cream are best made in an *electric blender*. Most cocktail bars use heavy-duty blenders designed for breaking up ice cubes, but the household blender works more efficiently if the ice is crushed (see page 21) before it is blended.

A *refrigerator* is essential – a warm cocktail is nasty. Keep the freezer compartment filled with ice trays and, where possible, use ice straight from the freezer. Otherwise store the ice in a well-insulated *ice bucket*.

All cocktails should be carefully measured, and as long as the *measure* remains constant throughout a recipe, the drink will have the correct flavour and consistency. A sharp *fruit knife* and a *chopping board* should be available for slicing garnishes and making twists of citrus peel (see page 9), and a *lemon squeezer* will be needed to extract lemon, lime and orange juices. You will increase the yield of citrus juice by soaking the fruit in hot water for a few minutes before squeezing it.

There are numerous other tools of the trade which are fun to collect, but armed with the equipment listed above, you should be able to mix any cocktail.

GLASSES

Almost any receptacle, from a brandy balloon to a pineapple shell, can be made to work effectively, provided that it is convincingly presented. As a rough guideline, however, choose stemmed glasses for cocktails which are not served on ice, as they will stay cool longer, and tumblers or highball glasses for rocks drinks. Short cocktails look their best in traditional triangular cocktail glasses, while goblet styles are generally used for drinks incorporating egg yolks.

All cocktails are served very cold and it makes a tremendous difference if the glasses have been chilled. Ideally, the glasses should stand in the refrigerator for an hour or two before needed, but a scoop of ice placed in the glass, and left there while the drink is being prepared, will chill it very efficiently.

GARNISHES

A garnish should enhance a drink without disguising it. It can be anything from a creamy-white orchid floating on an exotic frappéed concoction, to a stuffed green olive, speared on a cocktail stick and submerged in a classic Dry Martini.

Slices of lemon, orange and lime are the most frequently used garnishes, along with cocktail cherries which, incidentally, look prettier threaded on coloured cocktail sticks than merely dropped into the drink.

Let your imagination run riot when garnishing tropical cocktails, for truly beautiful creations can be dreamed up using exotic fruits like pineapple, mango or kiwi fruit.

One stylish method of decoration uses the fruit to reflect the ingredients of the drink – apricot wedges on the rim of the Apricot Sour glass, strawberries in a Strawberry Dawn or slices of peach with a Peach Daiquiri. Never go overboard, however, or the drink will look like a fruit salad.

Savoury garnishes include pearl onions, cucumber slices and slivers of the dark green skin, celery sticks, stuffed olives and sprigs of fresh mint. Celery salt and paprika are sometimes sprinkled over the finished drink before serving.

A pretty way to enhance a sweet cocktail is to frost the rim of the glass with sugar. First dip the rim into a saucer of egg white and then into one of finely granulated sugar. A pink frosting can be achieved by substituting grenadine for egg white. A Margarita is usually served in a salt-frosted glass. To salt the rim, hold the glass upside down and run a wedge of lime or lemon around it. Dip it in a saucer of salt and shake off the excess. Label sugar and salt clearly!

Cream and egg mixtures are flattered by a light dusting of freshly grated nutmeg or powdered cinnamon, while blanched almonds and crystallised stem ginger are both unusual and appealing when used with a little flair. Tropical cocktails look extra-special if frivolous extravagances such as coloured paper parasols are added, and straws come in all sorts of colours, shapes and sizes, and it is worth having a good selection. Never overdress a drink as it simply looks silly, but tantalise both the eye and the palate and you will have a successful cocktail.

TO MEASURE

Provided that the measure used is consistent throughout any one recipe, the drink will have the correct flavour, texture and colour. I have listed the ingredients as ratios which means that any measure, from a teaspoon to an egg cup, can be used effectively, depending on the size of, or number of drinks required.

TO SHAKE

If a recipe indicates that a drink is to be shaken, put the ingredients together with plenty of ice into the shaker and shake rapidly, with a vertical movement, until the outside of the shaker is frosty. Always strain unless specifically directed otherwise. NEVER shake fizzy ingredients – they are always added afterwards.

TO BLEND

Blend the ingredients stated with the recommended amount of crushed ice, and for only a few seconds or the drink becomes weak and watery.

TO MAKE 'GOMME' SYRUP

Dissolve a cup of white sugar in a cup of water by slowly bringing them to the boil and simmering for a couple of minutes. When cool, decant the sugar syrup into a bottle, label and store in a refrigerator.

TO EXTRACT CITRUS JUICE

Fresh fruit juice is infinitely better than bottled or canned, and to extract as much juice as possible from the fruit, soak for a few minutes in hot water before squeezing.

USING EGG WHITE

Egg white does not alter the flavour of a drink, it simply enhances its appearance, and only needs to be used in very small quantities. Separate one or two egg whites into a jug and literally 'cut' them with a sharp knife. This will prevent the whole lot slipping into the shaker when you only want a dash. (Keeps for two days if stored, covered, in a refrigerator.)

FLOATING A LIQUEUR

To float Galliano on a Harvey Wallbanger (see page 40) for example, pour the liqueur into a dessert spoon, hold the bowl of the spoon just above the drink and gently tip it so that the liqueur slips slowly onto the surface.

TO MAKE A TWIST OF PEEL

Using a very sharp knife, shave off strips of the coloured part of the peel leaving behind the white pith. Twist a strip of peel over the surface of the drink, which will release a fine spray of essential oil into the glass. Then drop the twist into the cocktail.

TO SERVE

Always hold the glass by the stem or the base to avoid fingerprints and unnecessary warming of the drink. Never fill the glass to the brim, and remember to leave room for a garnish if one is to be used.

TO MAKE CRUSHED ICE

Wrap ice cubes in a clean, dry tea towel and bash with a mallet.

Key to symbols used in text:	
Old fashioned	Goblet
Champagne flute	Highball
Cocktail glass	

ALEXANDER

Shake together equal parts of brandy, brown crème de cacao and cream, and dust with freshly-grated nutmeg.

AMERICAN BEAUTY

Shake together equal parts of brandy, grenadine, dry vermouth and orange juice, and a dash of white crème de menthe. Top with a little port.

BALTIMORE EGG NOG

Shake together two parts brandy, two parts Madeira, one part dark rum, two parts milk, an egg and a teaspoon of gomme syrup. Dust with grated nutmeg.

BANANA BLISS

Stir one part brandy with one part crème de banane.

BANDOS WOBBLER

A speciality of the Sand Bar, Bandos Island, Republic of the Maldives.
Shake together one part cognac, one part Campari, one part dark rum, one part orange juice and a dash of grenadine.

BETWEEN-THE-SHEETS

Shake together one part brandy, one part white rum, one part Cointreau and a dash of lemon juice.

BILLY HAMILTON

Shake together one part brandy, one part orange curaçao, one part brown crème de cacao and a dash of egg white.

BOMBAY

Stir two parts brandy with one part dry vermouth, one part sweet vermouth, a dash of pastis and a couple of dashes of orange curaçao.

BOSOM CARESSER

Shake together two parts brandy, one part orange curaçao, an egg yolk and a teaspoon of grenadine.

BRANDY CRUSTA

Shake together three parts brandy, one part orange curaçao, three dashes of maraschino, a dash of lemon juice and a dash of Angostura bitters. Serve with straws in a sugar-frosted glass, garnished with a cherry.

BRANDY FLIP

Shake a measure of brandy with a whole egg and a teaspoon of gomme syrup. Dust with grated nutmeg.

BRANDY GUMP

Shake together one part brandy, one part lemon juice and a couple of dashes of grenadine.

BRANDY PUNCH

Over a scoop of crushed ice, pour a measure of brandy and four dashes of curaçao. Stir, top up with dry ginger ale, and garnish with a sprig of mint and a slice of orange.

BREAKFAST NOG

Shake together one part brandy, one part orange curaçao, one egg and two parts milk. Dust with grated nutmeg.

Brandy Punch (above) and Green Room (facing page

CARNIVAL

Shake together equal parts brandy, apricot brandy and Lillet, a dash of kirsch and a dash of orange juice.

CHAMPS ELYSEES

Shake together three parts brandy, one part yellow Chartreuse, one part lemon juice and a dash of Angostura bitters.

CHERRY BLOSSOM

Shake together two parts brandy, three parts cherry brandy, a dash of curaçao, a dash of grenadine and a dash of lemon juice.

CHOCOLATE SOLDIER

Shake together equal parts brandy, dry vermouth and crème de cacao, and a couple of dashes of orange bitters.

CLASSIC

Shake together three parts brandy, one part lemon juice, one part orange curaçao and one part maraschino. Serve in a sugar-frosted glass with a twist of lemon peel.

COOL BREEZE

Shake together two parts brandy, one part Grand Marnier, six parts cream, a couple of dashes of maraschino cherry juice and a dash of Angostura bitters.

CUBAN

Shake together two parts brandy, one part apricot brandy and one part fresh lime juice.

DEPTH CHARGE

Shake together one part brandy, one part calvados, a couple of dashes of grenadine and four dashes of lemon juice.

EGG NOG

Shake together one part brandy, one part dark rum, one egg and one tablespoon of gomme syrup. Pour into a goblet, stir in two parts milk, and dust with grated nutmeg.

EGG SOUR

Shake together one part brandy, one part orange curaçao, the juice of a lemon, an egg and a teaspoon of gomme syrup.

FERNET

Stir one part brandy with one part Fernet Branca, a dash of Angostura bitters and a couple of dashes of gomme syrup. Add a twist of lemon peel.

FIRST NIGHT

Shake together two parts brandy, one part Van der Hum, one part Tia Maria and a teaspoon of cream.

GOLDEN GLEAM

Shake together two parts brandy, two parts Grand Marnier, one part lemon juice and one part orange juice.

GOLDEN MEDALLION

Shake together equal parts brandy, Galliano and fresh orange juice, and a dash of egg white. Grate a little zest of orange over the drink.

GREEN ROOM

Stir one part brandy with two parts dry vermouth and two dashes of orange curaçao.

HOOPLA

Shake together equal parts brandy, Cointreau, Lillet and lemon juice.

HORSE'S NECK

Drop a lemon spiral into a tall glass, anchor with ice cubes, add a measure of brandy and top with dry ginger ale.

LEVIATHAN

Shake together two parts brandy, one part sweet vermouth and one part orange juice.

MINT ROYAL

Shake together equal parts brandy, Royal Mint Chocolate Liqueur and lemon juice, and an egg white.

MORNING GLORY

Shake together two parts brandy, one part orange curaçao, one part lemon juice, and a couple of dashes each of Angostura bitters and pastis. Add a twist of lemon peel.

OLYMPIC

Shake together equal parts brandy, orange curaçao and orange juice.

PLAYMATE

Shake together equal parts brandy, apricot brandy, Grand Marnier and orange squash, an egg white and a dash of Angostura bitters. Add a twist of orange peel.

PRINCE CHARLES

Shake together equal parts brandy, Drambuie and lemon juice.

(Above) Brandy Crusta, Classic, Alexander, Horses Neck and Chocolate Soldier and (facing page) TNT

ROSS ROYAL

Shake together equal parts brandy, crème de banane and Royal Mint Chocolate Liqueur.

SIDECAR

Shake together two parts brandy, one part Cointreau and one part lemon juice.

STINGER

Stir two parts brandy with one part white crème de menthe and serve straight up or on the rocks.

THREE MILER

Shake together two parts brandy, one part white rum, a teaspoon of grenadine and a dash of lemon juice.

TNT

Stir two parts brandy with one part orange curaçao, a dash of Angostura bitters and a dash of pastis.

TOREADOR

Shake together two parts brandy, one part Kahlua and a dash of egg white.

WHIP

Shake together equal parts brandy, pastis, dry vermouth and curaçao.

ALASKA

Shake together three parts gin and one part yellow Chartreuse.

ALEXANDER

Shake together equal parts gin, brown crème de cacao and fresh cream, and serve in a sugar-frosted glass.

ANGEL FACE

Shake together equal parts gin, apricot brandy and calvados.

BARTENDER

Stir equal parts gin, sherry, Dubonnet and dry vermouth with a dash of Grand Marnier.

BERMUDIANA ROSE

Shake together two parts gin, and one part each of apricot brandy, grenadine and lemon juice.

BLUE BOTTLE

Stir two parts gin with one part blue curaçao, and one part passion fruit juice.

BLUE JACKET

Stir two parts gin with one part blue curaçao and one part orange bitters.

BLUE LADY

Shake together two parts blue curaçao, one part gin, one part fresh lemon juice and a dash of egg white.

BLUE STAR

Shake together two parts gin, two parts blue curaçao, one part Lillet and one part orange juice.

BYRRH SPECIAL

Stir one part gin with one part Byrrh.

CARIBBEAN SUNSET

Shake together equal parts of gin, crème de banane, blue curaçao, fresh cream and fresh lemon juice. Pour the creamy-blue mixture into a glass and splash with a little grenadine.

CARUSO

Stir one part gin with one part dry vermouth and one part green crème de menthe.

CASINO

Shake together two parts gin, one part maraschino, one part fresh lemon juice and a dash of orange bitters, and garnish with a cherry.

COASTER

Coat the inside of a glass with Angostura bitters by swirling a few drops round the bowl and tipping out the excess. Add gin to taste and top with soda water.

COLLINS–JOHN or TOM

Over cracked ice in a tall glass pour the juice of a lemon, a measure of gin and a teaspoon of fine sugar or gomme syrup. Top up with soda water, stir and garnish with a slice of lemon.

CROSS BOW

Shake together equal parts gin, Cointreau and crème de cacao.

CUPID'S BOW

Shake together equal parts gin, Forbidden Fruit liqueur, Aurum and passion fruit juice.

DRY MARTINI

There is no hard and fast rule governing the proportions of gin and dry vermouth which make up this drink. Three parts gin to one part dry vermouth stirred with lots of ice in a mixing glass, strained into a chilled cocktail glass with a plain or stuffed green olive, and zest of lemon peel squeezed over the top…is delicious. Orange bitters can be added, the ratio can be changed, and the drink can be served on the rocks. The glass can be rinsed out with vermouth and then gin added – you will only discover the most appealing drink by experimenting.

DUBONNET

Stir together equal parts gin and Dubonnet and add a twist of lemon peel.

DUBONNET ROYAL

Stir two parts Dubonnet with one part gin, a dash of Angostura bitters and a dash of orange curaçao. Splash with a dash of pastis and decorate with a cherry on a stick.

White Lady (above) and Blue Star (facing page)

FAIRY BELLE

Shake together three parts gin, one part apricot brandy, an egg white and a teaspoon of grenadine.

FALLEN ANGEL

Shake together three parts gin, one part fresh lemon juice, a couple of dashes of crème de menthe and a dash of Angostura bitters.

FLUFFY DUCK

Into an ice-filled glass pour two parts gin, two parts advocaat, one part Cointreau and one part orange juice. Stir in soda water to top up and serve with straws.

FOURTH DEGREE

Stir equal parts gin, dry vermouth and sweet vermouth, with a couple of dashes of pastis.

Tropical Dawn, Blue Lady, Green
Dragon, Pink Lady and Alaska

FRENCH 75

Shake together equal parts gin and fresh lemon juice, and a little gomme syrup. Pour over ice cubes and top up with chilled champagne.

GIBSON

Basically an extremely dry martini where only a dash of vermouth dilutes the gin – this drink can be served straight up or on the rocks and is garnished with a pearl (silverskin) onion.

GIMLET

Stir two parts gin with one part lime juice cordial and pour over ice cubes – top up with soda water if a long, sparkling drink is preferred.

GIN AND IT

Stir equal parts gin and sweet vermouth and garnish with a cherry.

GOLDEN DAWN

Shake together equal parts gin, calvados, apricot brandy and orange juice. Serve splashed with a little grenadine.

GRAPEFRUIT

Shake together equal parts gin and grapefruit juice, and a dash of gomme syrup.

GREEN DRAGON

Shake together four parts gin, two parts green crème de menthe and one part each of Kümmel and lemon juice.

HAVANA

Shake together one part gin, two parts apricot brandy, one part Swedish punsch and a dash of lemon juice.

HAWAIIAN

Shake together equal parts gin and orange juice, and a dash of orange curaçao.

HIBERNIAN SPECIAL

Shake together equal parts gin, Cointreau and green curaçao, and a dash of lemon juice.

INSPIRATION

Stir equal parts gin, dry vermouth, calvados and Grand Marnier.

ITZA PARAMOUNT

Stir two parts gin with one part Drambuie and one part Cointreau.

LONG ISLAND TEA

Over ice cubes pour one part gin, one part vodka, one part light rum and two parts cold tea. Top up with cola, stir and garnish with a sprig of mint and a slice of lemon.

MAIDEN'S PRAYER

Shake together three parts gin, three parts Cointreau, one part orange juice and one part lemon juice.

MAINBRACE

Shake together equal parts gin, Cointreau and grapefruit juice.

MEDITERRANEAN

Over ice cubes pour two parts gin and one part blue curaçao. Top up with lemonade.

French 75 (above) and Silver Streak (facing page)

NEGRONI

Over ice cubes pour equal parts gin, sweet vermouth and Campari. Garnish with a slice of orange and top up with soda water if required.

OLD ETONIAN

Stir one part gin with one part Lillet, a couple of dashes of crème de noyau and a splash of orange bitters. Garnish with a twist of orange peel.

OPERA

Stir four parts gin with one part Dubonnet and one part maraschino. Garnish with a twist of orange peel.

PERFECT LADY

Shake together two parts gin, one part peach brandy, one part fresh lemon juice and the white of an egg.

PERFECT MARTINI

A less dry martini, this is made with two parts gin and half a part each of dry and sweet vermouth. Stir with plenty of ice in a mixing glass, strain into a stemmed cocktail glass and add a twist of lemon peel.

PINK GIN

This is made in the same way as a *Coaster* but served with iced water rather than soda.

PINK LADY

Shake together four parts gin, one part grenadine and an egg white. Garnish with a maraschino cherry.

PRINCETON

Stir two parts gin with one part port and a dash of orange bitters. Add a twist of lemon peel.

QUEENS

Shake together equal parts gin, dry vermouth, sweet vermouth and pineapple juice.

SIFI FLIP

Shake together two parts gin, one part Cointreau, one part grenadine, one part lemon juice and an egg yolk.

SILVER JUBILEE

Shake together two parts gin, one part crème de banane and one part cream.

SILVER STREAK

Stir three parts gin with two parts Kümmel and serve straight up or on the rocks.

SINGAPORE SLING

Stir two parts gin with one part cherry brandy and one part lemon juice. Pour over ice cubes, add soda water to taste and garnish with a sprig of mint and a slice of orange.

STRAWBERRY DAWN

This delicious, summery concoction is made with fresh strawberries: Blend one part gin with one part coconut cream, three fresh strawberries and a couple of scoops of crushed ice – the secret is not to blend for too long or the drink becomes over-diluted. Serve in a large, bowl-shaped glass and stick a strawberry on the rim. To be drunk through short, fat straws.

SWEET MARTINI

Stir two parts gin with one part sweet vermouth and garnish with a cherry.

TANGO

Shake together two parts gin, one part sweet vermouth, one part dry vermouth, a couple of dashes of orange curaçao and a dash of orange juice.

TROPICAL DAWN

Shake two parts gin with two parts fresh orange juice, pour over a scoop of crushed ice and trickle one part Campari over the top. Serve with short straws.

VISITOR

Shake together equal parts gin, Cointreau and crème de banane, a dash of orange juice and an egg white.

WESTERN ROSE

Shake together two parts gin, one part apricot brandy and one part dry vermouth, and a dash of lemon juice.

WHITE HEATHER

Shake together three parts gin, one part Cointreau, one part dry vermouth and one part pineapple juice.

WHITE LADY

Shake together two parts gin, one part Cointreau, one part lemon juice and a dash of egg white.

ANTILLANO

Shake together equal parts golden rum, white rum, pineapple juice and grapefruit juice, a dash of Angostura bitters and a teaspoon of grenadine. Pour over crushed ice, garnish imaginatively and serve with fat straws.

APRICOT LADY

Blend together two parts golden rum, two parts apricot brandy, one part fresh lime juice, three dashes of orange curaçao, a couple of dashes of egg white and a small scoop of crushed ice. Serve with a slice of orange and short straws.

BACARDI COCKTAIL

Shake together three parts white rum, one part fresh lemon or lime juice and a few drops of grenadine.

BAHAMAS

Shake together one part white rum, one part Southern Comfort, one part fresh lemon juice and a dash of crème de banane.

BANANA DAIQUIRI

Blend together three parts white rum, one part crème de banane, the juice of half a lime, half a banana and two scoops of crushed ice. Don't blend for too long or the drink will become over-diluted. Pile the icy sorbet into a large goblet and serve with fat straws.

BARRACUDA

Shake together two parts golden rum, one part Galliano, two parts pineapple juice, a couple of dashes of gomme syrup and a good squeeze of lime juice. Serve in a large goblet or, ideally, a pineapple shell, top with champagne and garnish with a slice of lime and a cherry.

BLUE HAWAIIAN

This truly tropical cocktail is made in a blender. Blend together two parts white rum, one part blue curaçao, four parts pineapple juice, two parts coconut cream and a scoop of crushed ice.

CASABLANCA

Blend together three parts white rum, four parts pineapple juice, two parts coconut cream, a couple of dashes of grenadine and two scoops of crushed ice. Serve with straws.

COCONUT DAIQUIRI

Shake together one part white rum, two parts coconut liqueur, four parts fresh lime juice and a dash of egg white.

CRÈME DE RHUM

Shake together equal parts white rum, crème de banane and orange squash, and a dash of cream. Garnish with a cherry and a slice of orange.

CUBA LIBRE

Over ice cubes pour one part white rum and the juice of half a lime. Drop in the lime shell and stir in cola to taste. Serve with straws.

DAIQUIRI

Shake together three parts white rum, one

part fresh lime juice and three dashes of gomme (or Falernum) syrup. (If limes are unavailable, substitute lemons.)

DAIQUIRI BLOSSOM

Shake together one part white rum, one part fresh orange juice and a dash of maraschino.

DAIQUIRI LIBERAL

Stir two parts white rum with one part sweet vermouth and a dash of Amer Picon.

DEAN'S GATE

Stir two parts white rum with one part Drambuie and one part lime juice cordial. Add a twist of orange peel.

FROSTY DAWN

Shake together two parts white rum, one part maraschino, one part Falernum syrup and two parts orange juice.

FROZEN DAIQUIRI

Blend together one part white rum, a dash of maraschino, the juice of half a lime, a dash of gomme syrup, and two scoops of crushed ice. Serve with fat straws.

JAMAICA JOE

Shake together equal parts Jamaica rum, Tia Maria and advocaat. Add a dash of grenadine and dust with nutmeg.

Night Light (above), Frozen Daiquiri (facing page)

LA FLORIDA DAIQUIRI

Blend together two measures light rum, one teaspoon gomme syrup or fine sugar, one teaspoon maraschino liqueur, the juice of a lime and a small scoop of crushed ice. Serve with short straws.

LITTLE PRINCESS

Stir one part white rum with one part sweet vermouth.

MAI TAI

This fine drink was invented by *Trader Vic*, and his own blended 'Mai Tai' rum is used in the following recipe:
1 lime, 2 ounces Trader Vic Mai Tai rum, ½ ounce orange curaçao, ¼ ounce rock candy syrup, ¼ ounce orgeat syrup.
Cut the lime in half and squeeze the juice over shaved (crushed) ice in a large old-fashioned tumbler. Add the remaining ingredients and enough shaved ice to fill the glass. Garnish with one spent lime shell, a sprig of fresh mint and a cherry and a pineapple chunk on a stick. Serve with straws. 'Mai Tai' means 'The Best' in Tahitian.

Jamaica Joe, Palm Breeze, Rum Cooler, Yellow Bird and Blue Hawaiian

MALLORCA

Stir three parts white rum with one part dry vermouth, one part crème de banane and one part Drambuie.

MARY PICKFORD

Shake together one part white rum, one part pineapple juice, a teaspoon of grenadine and a dash of maraschino.

MOLOKAI MIKE

A *Trader Vic* original.
Blend together 1 ounce orange juice, 1 ounce lemon juice, $\frac{1}{2}$ ounce orgeat syrup, $\frac{1}{2}$ ounce brandy, 1 ounce light rum and one small scoop crushed ice. Pour into glass. Blend together $\frac{1}{2}$ ounce Rhum Negrita, a dash of grenadine and half a scoop crushed ice. Slowly pour into top half of the glass.

MOOMBA COCKTAIL

Shake together three parts white rum, three parts Grand Marnier, two parts orange juice, one part lemon juice and a dash of grenadine. Add a twist of orange peel.

NEVADA

Shake together two parts dark rum, two parts grapefruit juice, one part fresh lime juice and one part gomme syrup.

NIGHT LIGHT

Shake together two parts white rum, one part orange curaçao and an egg yolk.

PALM BREEZE

Shake together three parts dark rum, two parts yellow Chartreuse, one part crème de cacao, the juice of half a fresh lime and a dash of grenadine.

PEACH DAIQUIRI

Blend together three parts white rum, one part peach brandy, the juice of half a lime, half a fresh, peeled peach and two scoops of crushed ice. Pile into a goblet and garnish with a wedge of peach. Serve with short straws.

PETITE FLEUR

Shake together equal parts white rum, Cointreau and fresh grapefruit juice.

PINA COLADA

This is one of the most popular of tropical cocktails. Blend together three parts white or golden rum, four parts pineapple juice, two parts coconut cream and two scoops of crushed ice. Serve in a tumbler or even better, a pineapple husk. Garnish with fruit, paper parasols etc., and two straws.

PINEAPPLE FIZZ

Shake together two parts white rum, one part pineapple juice and a teaspoon of gomme syrup. Strain and top up with half lemonade and half soda water.

PLANTERS

Shake together one part golden rum, one part orange juice and a dash of fresh lemon juice.

PLANTERS' PUNCH

Over ice cubes pour one part golden (or dark) rum, one part fresh lime (or lemon) juice, a dash of Angostura bitters and two teaspoons of grenadine. Top up with soda water and stir. Decorate with slices of orange and lemon.

RUM COOLER

Shake together one part dark rum, the juice of a lemon (or lime), and four dashes of grenadine. Add ice and top up with soda water.

SCORPION

Blend together three parts golden rum, two parts fresh lemon juice, two parts fresh orange juice, one part brandy, a couple of dashes of orgeat syrup and a scoop of crushed ice. Pour the mixture over more crushed ice, garnish with a sprig of mint and a slice of orange and serve with short straws.

SHANGHAI

Shake together four parts dark rum, one part pastis, three parts lemon juice and a couple of dashes of grenadine.

SIX BELLS

Shake together two parts dark rum, one part orange curaçao, one part fresh lime juice, a couple of dashes of Angostura bitters and a dash of gomme syrup.

Pineapple Fizz (above) and Blue Hawaiian (facing page)

STRAWBERRY DAIQUIRI

Blend together three parts white rum, one part fraise liqueur, the juice of half a lime, three strawberries and two scoops of crushed ice. Pile into a large, bowl-shaped glass and garnish with a strawberry.

SWEET MEMORIES

Stir one part white rum with one part dry vermouth and one part orange curaçao.

TRINIDAD PUNCH

Shake together three parts dark rum, two parts fresh lime juice, a teaspoon of gomme syrup and a couple of dashes of Angostura bitters. Pour over ice cubes, drop in a twist of lemon peel and dust with nutmeg.

YELLOW BIRD

Shake together three parts white rum, one part Galliano, one part Cointreau and one part fresh lime juice. Do not strain – simply pour into a stemmed glass and garnish with a slice of lime.

ALVEAR PALACE

Shake together five parts vodka, two parts pineapple juice and one part apricot brandy.

APRÈS SKI

Shake together equal parts vodka, green crème de menthe and Pernod. Top up with lemonade, decorate with a sprig of mint and a slice of lemon, and serve with straws.

BALALAIKA

Shake together equal parts of vodka, Cointreau and lemon juice.

BARBARA

Shake together two parts vodka, one part crème de cacao and one part cream.

BLACK RUSSIAN

Over ice cubes pour two parts vodka and one part Kahlua.

BLENHEIM

Shake together two parts vodka, one part Tia Maria and one part fresh orange juice.

BLOODSHOT

Shake together one part vodka, two parts beef bouillon or condensed consommé, two parts tomato juice, a dash of lemon juice, a couple of dashes of Worcestershire sauce and a pinch of celery salt.

BLOODY MARY

Shake together one part vodka, four parts tomato juice, a couple of dashes of Worcestershire sauce, a dash of lemon juice and a pinch of celery salt. Add Tabasco and pepper to taste and serve with a stick of celery which may be used to stir the drink.

BLUE LAGOON

Over ice cubes pour one part vodka, one part blue curaçao and top up with lemonade.

CHI CHI

Blend together three parts vodka, two parts coconut cream, eight parts pineapple juice and two scoops of crushed ice. Garnish with a slice of fresh pineapple and a cherry and serve with fat straws.

COSSACK

Shake together equal parts vodka, brandy and lime juice, and a teaspoon of gomme syrup.

CZARINE

Stir two parts vodka with one part dry vermouth, one part apricot brandy and a dash of Angostura bitters.

(Above) Godmother, Moscow Mule, Blue Lagoon, Vodkatini and Cossack and Road Runner (facing page)

DANIELLI

Stir two parts vodka with one part dry vermouth and a couple of dashes of Campari. Add a twist of lemon peel.

DEB'S DELIGHT

Stir two parts vodka with two parts apricot brandy and one part anisette. Do not strain but pour liquid and ice into a tumbler and top with cream.

FROZEN STEPPES

Blend together two parts vodka, one part brown creme de cacao and a scoop of vanilla ice cream.

GIPSY

Shake together two parts vodka, one part Bénédictine and a dash of Angostura bitters.

GODMOTHER

Over ice cubes pour two parts vodka and one part amaretto.

GOLDEN TANG

Shake together four parts vodka, two parts Strega, one part crème de banane and one part orange squash. Garnish with a cherry.

HARVEY WALLBANGER

Over ice cubes pour three parts vodka and eight parts orange juice. Float two teaspoons of Galliano on top and garnish with a slice of orange.

HONG KONG FIZZ

Shake together equal parts of vodka, gin, yellow Chartreuse, green Chartreuse, Bénédictine and lemon juice. Top up with soda water and garnish with slices of lemon, orange and lime, and a cherry.

JUSTINE

Shake together two parts vodka, one part crème de noyau, one part kirsch, a couple of dashes of orgeat syrup and two parts cream.

KATINKA

Shake together three parts vodka, two parts apricot brandy and one part fresh lime juice. Pour over a scoop of crushed ice and garnish with a sprig of mint.

LUCKY DIP

Shake together two parts vodka, one part crème de banane, one part lemon squash and an egg white.

MOSCOW MULE

Over ice cubes pour two parts vodka and one part fresh lime (or lemon) juice. Stir in ginger beer to top up, garnish with a sprig of mint and a slice of lime, and serve with straws.

ORANGE BLOSSOM

Shake together two parts vodka, two parts apricot brandy, one part Galliano and one part orange juice. Top up with ginger ale, garnish with a slice of orange and a cherry, and serve with straws.

PATRICIA

Stir one part vodka with one part sweet vermouth and one part orange curaçao. Add a twist of lemon peel.

QUIET SUNDAY

Shake together two parts vodka, one part amaretto and eight parts orange juice. Pour into an ice-filled glass and splash in a few drops of grenadine.

ROAD RUNNER

Shake together two parts vodka, one part amaretto and one part coconut milk. Dust with grated nutmeg.

ROBERTA MAY

Shake together equal parts vodka, Aurum and orange squash, and a dash of egg white.

SALTY DOG

Over ice cubes in a salt-frosted glass pour one part vodka and two parts grapefruit juice.

SCOTCH FROG

Shake together two parts vodka, one part Galliano, one part Cointreau, the juice of a lime, a dash of Angostura bitters and a teaspoon of maraschino cherry juice.

SCREWDRIVER

Over ice cubes pour one part vodka and four parts orange juice.

SEA BREEZE

Stir three parts vodka with one part dry vermouth, one part blue curaçao and one part Galliano. Pour over ice cubes and add a twist of orange peel.

SERENISSIMA

Shake together one part vodka, one part fresh grapefruit juice and a dash of Campari. Pour into an ice-filled glass.

SILVER SUNSET

Shake together two parts vodka, one part apricot brandy, one part lemon juice, six parts orange juice, a dash of Campari and a dash of egg white. Pour over ice cubes, garnish with a slice of orange and a cherry, and serve with straws.

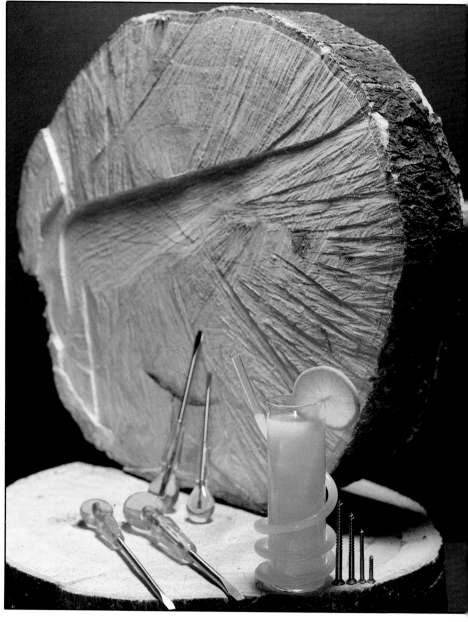

Screwdriver (above) and Hong Kong Fizz (facing page)

SNAKE-IN-THE-GRASS

Over ice cubes pour two parts vodka and one part crème de menthe. Top up with lemonade and garnish with a slice of orange.

VODKATINI

As with the gin-based dry Martini, there are countless variations as to the proportions used in this drink. A safe ratio is two parts vodka to one part dry vermouth, to which a twist of lemon peel is added.

YELLOW FINGERS

Shake together two parts vodka, two parts Southern Comfort, two parts orange juice and one part Galliano. Top up with lemonade and garnish with a slice of orange and a maraschino cherry.

AFFINITY
Stir two parts Scotch with one part sweet vermouth and a couple of dashes of Angostura bitters.

ANGERS ROSE
Shake equal parts bourbon, Cointreau and pineapple juice with a dash of Campari and a dash of egg white. Garnish with a slice of orange and a cherry.

BARBICAN
Shake together seven parts Scotch, one part Drambuie and two parts passion fruit juice.

BOBBY BURNS
Stir one part Scotch with one part sweet vermouth and three dashes of Bénédictine.

BOSTON FLIP
Shake equal parts rye and Madeira with one egg yolk and a teaspoon of gomme syrup.

BOURBONELLA
Stir two parts bourbon with one part dry vermouth, one part orange curaçao and a dash of grenadine.

BROOKLYN
Stir equal parts rye and sweet vermouth with a dash of maraschino and a dash of Amer Picon.

COMMODORE
Shake four parts rye with one part fresh lime juice and two dashes of orange bitters. Add sugar if required.

DAILY MAIL
Shake equal parts rye, Amer Picon and orange squash with three dashes of orange bitters.

DANDY
Stir equal parts rye and Dubonnet with a dash of Angostura bitters and three dashes of Cointreau. Garnish with orange and lemon peel.

EMBASSY ROYAL
Shake together two parts bourbon, one part Drambuie, one part sweet vermouth and two dashes of orange squash.

EMPIRE GLORY
Shake together two parts rye, one part ginger wine, one part fresh lemon juice and two dashes of grenadine.

EVANS
Stir a large measure of rye with a dash of apricot brandy and a dash of curaçao.

FORESTERS' DELIGHT
Shake together one part bourbon, one part Cointreau, two dashes of blue curaçao and two dashes of freshly squeezed lemon juice. Serve in a sugar-frosted glass, garnished with a cherry.

FRISCO SOUR
Shake together three parts bourbon, one part Bénédictine, one part fresh lemon juice and one part fresh lime juice. Garnish with slices of lemon and lime.

GODFATHER
Over ice cubes pour two parts Scotch or bourbon and one part amaretto.

HOOTS MON
Stir two parts Scotch with one part Lillet and one part sweet vermouth.

HUNTER
Stir two parts rye with one part cherry brandy.

INK STREET
Shake together equal parts rye, lemon juice and orange juice.

KENTUCKY SUNSET
Stir three parts bourbon with one part Strega and one part anisette. Garnish with a twist of orange peel.

LINSTEAD
Shake together one part Scotch, one part sweetened pineapple juice and a dash of pastis. Garnish with a twist of lemon peel.

LOS ANGELES
Shake together two parts Scotch, one part lemon juice, one egg and a dash of sweet vermouth.

MANHATTAN
The traditional Manhattan is made with two parts rye, one part sweet vermouth and a dash of Angostura bitters, stirred and garnished with a cherry. A Dry Manhattan replaces sweet vermouth with dry and the cherry with a twist of lemon peel; and a Perfect Manhattan uses half sweet and half dry vermouth and is garnished with both a cherry and a twist of lemon peel.

MAPLE LEAF
Shake together two parts bourbon, one part lemon juice and a teaspoon of maple syrup.

MERRY K
Stir two parts bourbon with one part orange curaçao and add a twist of lemon peel.

MINT JULEP
There is a delicate art to making this drink successfully: Into the glass put four or five fresh mint leaves, a tablespoon of finely ground sugar and a tablespoon of water and crush until the sugar is dissolved. Add a measure of bourbon and top up with crushed ice – which cause the outside of the glass to frost. Decorate with a sprig of fresh mint and serve with straws.

OLD FASHIONED
Over a teaspoon of sugar in the glass shake a couple of dashes of Angostura bitters and a little water. Stir to dissolve the sugar and fill the glass with ice. Top up with rye, decorate with a cherry and a twist of lemon peel or a slice of orange, and serve with a stirrer.

OLD PAL
Stir together equal parts rye, dry vermouth and Campari.

OPENING
Stir two parts rye with one part sweet vermouth and one part grenadine.

ORIENTAL
Shake together two parts rye, one part sweet vermouth, one part white curaçao and one part fresh lime juice.

PICCA
Stir two parts Scotch with one part Galliano and one part Punt e Mes, and decorate with a cherry.

ROB ROY
Stir together equal parts Scotch and sweet vermouth, and a dash of Angostura bitters. Garnish with a cherry.

ROYALIST
Stir one part bourbon with two parts dry vermouth, one part Bénédictine and a dash of peach bitters.

RUSTY NAIL
Over ice cubes pour two parts Scotch and one part Drambuie, and drop in a twist of lemon peel.

RYE LANE
Shake together equal parts rye, white curaçao and orange juice, and a couple of dashes of crème de noyau.

SHAMROCK
Stir one part Irish whiskey with one part dry vermouth, three dashes of green Chartreuse and three dashes of green crème de menthe.

SILENT THIRD
Shake together equal parts Scotch, Cointreau and lemon juice.

UP-TO-DATE
Stir two parts rye with two parts dry vermouth, one part Grand Marnier and a dash of Angostura bitters. Garnish with a twist of orange peel.

WARD EIGHT
Shake together two parts rye, one part orange juice, one part lemon juice and a teaspoon of grenadine.

WEMBLEY
Shake together equal parts Scotch, dry vermouth and pineapple juice.

WHISKY COCKTAIL
Stir four parts Scotch with one part orange curaçao and a couple of dashes of Angostura bitters. Garnish with a cherry.

WHISKY MAC
Into a glass pour three parts Scotch and two parts ginger wine.

WHISKY SOUR
Shake together three parts Scotch, two parts freshly squeezed lemon juice, one part gomme syrup and a dash of egg white. Garnish with a slice of lemon.

WHIZZ BANG
Stir two parts Scotch with one part dry vermouth, and a couple of dashes each of pastis, grenadine and orange bitters.

Hunter (facing page)

Bobby Burns
Whisky Mac
Shamrock
Barbican
Rob Roy

Sherry Cobbler, Kir, Champagne
Cocktail, Black Velvet and Sherry Flip

MIMOSA

Make in the same way as Buck's Fizz, and add a splash of orange curaçao.

PORT WINE

Stir four parts port with one part brandy and add a twist of orange peel.

RITZ FIZZ

Pour a dash each of amaretto, blue curaçao and clear lemon juice into the glass, top with chilled champagne and garnish with a rose petal.

SHERRY COBBLER

Put plenty of crushed ice into a glass and half-fill with sherry. Add a splash of orange curaçao and a teaspoon of gomme syrup and stir. Garnish with a sprig of mint and a slice each of orange and lemon.

SHERRY FLIP

Shake together a measure of sherry, a teaspoon of sugar and an egg. Grate a little nutmeg over the top.

SHERRY TWIST

Shake together two parts dry sherry, two

Americano (above) and Bucks Fizz (facing page)

parts orange juice, one part Scotch and a couple of dashes of Cointreau.

SPRITZER

Over two or three ice cubes pour equal parts dry white wine and soda water. Add twist of lemon peel.

VERMOUTH CASSIS

Over ice cubes pour equal parts crème de cassis and dry vermouth.

AFTER DINNER
Shake together equal parts of prunelle brandy, cherry brandy and lemon juice.

ANGEL'S TIP
Pour three parts brown crème de cacao into the glass, and float one part cream on top.

APRICOT SOUR
Shake together one part apricot brandy, two parts lemon juice, a dash of Angostura bitters, a dash of egg white and a dash of gomme syrup. Garnish with a wedge of apricot.

BANSHEE
Blend together three parts white crème de cacao, three parts crème de banane, four parts cream, a dash of gomme syrup and a small scoop of crushed ice.

BENTLEY
Stir one part applejack brandy with one part Dubonnet.

BLACKTHORN
Stir two parts sloe gin with one part sweet vermouth and a dash of orange bitters. Add a twist of lemon peel.

BLOCK AND FALL
Stir two parts Cointreau with two parts apricot brandy, one part anisette and one part applejack brandy (or calvados).

BLUE MARGARITA
Shake together two parts tequila, two parts freshly squeezed lime juice and one part blue curaçao.

BRAVE BULL
Over ice cubes pour equal measures of tequila and Kahlua.

BREWER STREET RASCAL
Shake together one part Mandarine Napoléon, four parts grapefruit juice, a splash of vodka and a dash of egg white. Garnish with a piece of grapefruit.

CALVADOS COCKTAIL
Shake together two parts calvados, two parts orange juice, one part Cointreau and one part orange bitters.

CLUBMAN
Shake together one part Irish Mist, four parts orange juice and a dash of egg white. Pour over ice cubes and slowly add a few drops of blue curaçao to marble the drink.

COOL BANANA
Shake together four parts crème de banane, three parts triple sec, one part grenadine, four parts double cream and a dash of egg white. Serve with fat straws.

DIKI DIKI
Shake together four parts calvados, one part Swedish punch and one part grapefruit juice.

DOCTOR
Shake together two parts Swedish punsch and one part fresh lemon or lime juice.

DUKE
Shake together two parts Drambuie, one part orange juice, one part lemon juice and an egg. Pour into the glass and splash in a little champagne.

FUTURITY
Stir one part sloe gin with one part sweet vermouth and a dash of Angostura bitters.

GINGER SQUARE
Over ice cubes pour a measure of ginger brandy and stir in ginger ale to taste.

GLOOM CHASER
Shake together equal parts of Grand Marnier, white curaçao, grenadine and lemon juice.

GOLDEN CADILLAC
Shake together equal parts Galliano, white crème de cacao and fresh cream.

GOLDEN DREAM
Shake together equal parts Galliano, Cointreau, orange juice and cream.

Viking (above) and Moon Drops (facing page)

GOLDEN SLIPPER
Shake together one part yellow Chartreuse, one part apricot brandy and an egg yolk.

GRAND SLAM
Stir two parts Swedish punsch with one part sweet vermouth and one part dry vermouth.

GRASSHOPPER
Shake together equal parts white crème de cacao, green crème de menthe and cream.

HARVEY COWPUNCHER
Over ice cubes pour a measure of Galliano and stir in fresh milk to taste.

HONEYMOON
Shake together one part Bénédictine, one part applejack brandy, one part lemon juice and three dashes of orange curaçao.

Duke, Harvey Cowpuncher, Golden Cadillac, Ritz Royale and Bentley

JACK ROSE

Shake together three parts applejack brandy, one part grenadine and the juice of half a lime.

KING ALFONSE

Pour three parts Kahlua into the glass, and float one part cream on top.

LIBERTY

Stir two parts applejack brandy with one part white rum and a dash of gomme syrup.

LIMBO

Fill the glass with ice cubes and pour in one part peach brandy and four parts pineapple juice.

LONDON FOG

Shake together one part white crème de menthe, one part anisette and a dash of Angostura bitters.

MACARONI

Shake together two parts pastis and one part sweet vermouth.

MANDARINE SOUR

Shake together one part Mandarine Napoléon, one part fresh lemon juice, a dash of egg white and a dash of Angostura bitters.

MARGARITA

Shake together two parts tequila, two parts fresh lime juice and one part triple sec. Serve in a salt-frosted glass.

MISTY COOLER

Shake together one part Irish Mist, two parts lemon juice, a dash of grenadine and a dash of of egg white. Pour over ice cubes and top with soda water.

MOCHA MINT

Shake together equal parts Kahlua, white crème de menthe and white crème de cacao. Pour over ice cubes.

MOCKINGBIRD

Over ice cubes pour one part tequila, two parts grapefruit juice and a dash of lime juice. Serve with a cherry and a stirrer.

MONA LISA

Shake together one part Amer Picon, one part orange curaçao, one part Bénédictine and a teaspoon of double cream. Dust with cinnamon.

MOON DROPS

A speciality of the Jamaica Hilton International.
Stir 1 ounce Christian Brothers Sherry with four ounces Red Stripe Beer and strain into a cocktail glass. Garnish with a melon ball.

NIGHTCAP FLIP

Shake together one part anisette, one part orange curaçao, one part brandy and an egg yolk.

ORANGE CADILLAC

This creamy, pale orange drink is made in a blender. Blend together four parts Galliano,

London Fog (above) and Honeymoon (facing page)

three parts white crème de cacao, one part fresh orange juice, four parts cream and a scoop of crushed ice.

PICON

Stir one part Amer Picon with one part sweet vermouth.

PIMM'S No. 1

A true Pimm's should not resemble an alcoholic fruit salad! Stir one part Pimm's No. 1 Cup with two or three parts lemonade, 7UP, Sprite or ginger ale. Add plenty of ice, a slice of lemon, a slice of orange, a slice of cucumber and, if available, a sprig of mint.

PINK PUSSY

Shake together two parts Campari, one part peach brandy and a dash of egg white.
Pour over ice cubes and top up with bitter lemon.

PISCO PUNCH

Shake together two parts pisco, one part pineapple juice, one part fresh lime juice, a couple of dashes of maraschino and a couple of dashes of gomme syrup.

POUSSE CAFÉ

A striped drink in a tall, thin glass, the Pousse Café is a true tester of the bartender's art. It consists of several coloured liqueurs, of different densities, floated one upon another, and any number between three and seven can be used. The liquids can be poured down the side of the glass or over the back of a teaspoon. There are several different combinations of which these are examples.
In the order stated pour equal quantities of the following: grenadine, crème de menthe,

Galliano, Kümmel and brandy; or grenadine, Parfait Amour and maraschino. An added indulgence is a dollop of thick, sweet cream on top . . .

RITZ ROYALE

Shake together equal parts peach brandy, Punt e Mes and fresh lemon juice, with a dash of gomme syrup. Strain and top up with soda water.

ROSE

Stir one part kirsch with two parts dry vermouth and a teaspoon of sirop de roses. Garnish with a cherry or a rose petal.

RUN RUN

A speciality of the Jamaica Hilton International.
Shake the following ingredients with crushed ice: 1¼ ounces Amontillado, 1 ounce crème de cacao, ½ ounce overproof rum, 3 ounces pineapple juice and ½ ounce grenadine. Do not strain, but pour into a large goblet or brandy balloon and garnish extravagantly.

SILK STOCKINGS

This drink is as smooth as it sounds, and made in a blender. Into the blender cup pour three parts tequila, two parts white crème de cacao, three parts fresh cream and a dash of grenadine. Whizz up with a scoop of crushed ice and pour the mixture into a glass. Dust with cinnamon and garnish with a cherry.

SLOE GIN COCKTAIL

Stir two parts sloe gin with one part dry vermouth and one part sweet vermouth.

SNOWBALL

Stir one part advocaat with a dash of lime juice cordial, and then gently stir in lemonade. Pour over ice cubes and garnish with a maraschino cherry.

TEQUILA SUNRISE

Over ice in a tall glass pour one part tequila and four parts orange juice. Stir and add two dashes of grenadine. Garnish with a slice of orange and a cherry and serve with straws.

VALENCIA

Shake together two parts apricot brandy, one part orange juice and four dashes of orange bitters. If this drink is topped up with ice-cold champagne, it becomes a *Valencia Smile.*

VELVET HAMMER

Shake together equal parts of Cointreau, Tia Maria and fresh cream.

VIKING

Shake together three parts Swedish punsch, one part aquavit and one part fresh lime juice. Pour over ice cubes.

WATERLOO

Over ice in a tall glass pour one part Mandarine Napoléon and four parts fresh orange juice.

WINNIE-THE-POOH

Shake together four parts egg flip, one part coffee liqueur, one part chocolate liqueur and two parts fresh cream.

For anyone preferring not to drink alcohol, the following drinks succeed on three counts: they tempt the eye, they tempt the palate and they taste delicious. The Pussyfoot (far left) not only tastes good, but it is healthy too, combining orange, lemon and lime juices with egg yolk and grenadine (which adds sweetness and colour) and, here, it is made into a long drink by topping up the glass with soda water. A Jersey Lily (second from left) is basically fizzy apple juice with a dash of Angostura bitters, and the San Francisco (third from left) is another of the refreshing fruit juice and grenadine concoctions. Ice cream, fresh cream and cola add up to a Mickey Mouse (centre front), while the Capucine (third from right) is another creamy mixture, this time flavoured with peppermint and topped with grated chocolate. The Princess Margaret (second from right) is virtually a strawberry sorbet, served in a sugar-frosted glass, the rim of the glass dipped in sirop de fraise and then in granulated sugar. The marzipan-like taste of the Yellow Dwarf (far right) comes from orgeat – a non-alcoholic, almond-flavoured syrup.

Mocktails

'Temperance is the noblest gift of the gods' (Euripides), and 'Temperance is the greatest of all the virtues' (Plutarch). And who are we to argue? Syrups in flavours as diverse as peach, almond, strawberry and mint, as well as a wide range of exotic fruit juices mean that mocktails can be just as exciting and delicious as their alcoholic rivals. Here is the chance to go a little bit mad with the garnishes – so let your imagination run riot!

ACAPULCO GOLD

Shake together six parts pineapple juice, one part grapefruit juice, two parts coconut cream, two parts fresh cream and a scoop of crushed ice. Serve unstrained.

ANITA

Shake together three parts orange juice, one part lemon juice and a couple of dashes of Angostura bitters. Top with soda water, garnish with fruit and serve with straws.

APPLEADE

Chop up two large apples and pour a pint of boiling water over them. Sprinkle in about a teaspoon of sugar and leave to stand for a few minutes. Strain the liquid and leave to cool. Serve with plenty of ice and garnish with a wedge of apple and a slice of lemon.

BARLEYADE

Pour equal quantities of lemon barley and lemonade into a tumbler; add ice, a slice of lemon, and straws.

BOO BOO'S SPECIAL

Shake together equal quantities of orange juice and pineapple juice, a squeeze of lemon juice, a dash of Angostura bitters, a dash of grenadine and a scoop of crushed ice. Serve unstrained, garnish with fruit and top with a little water if desired.

CAPUCINE

Shake together one part peppermint cordial and four parts fresh cream. Strain and add crushed ice. Finely grate a little plain chocolate over the top.

CINDERELLA

Shake together equal parts pineapple juice, orange juice and lemon juice. Strain over ice cubes, top with soda water and splash in a little grenadine. Garnish with a slice of pineapple, or a pineapple chunk and a cherry on a stick, and serve with straws.

EGG NOG

Shake together a tumbler-full of milk, an egg, a teaspoon of sugar and ice. Dust with freshly-grated nutmeg, garnish with a maraschino cherry and serve with straws.

GODCHILD

Place four or five ice cubes in the glass and fill three-quarters full with lemonade. Add a squeeze of lemon juice and gently pour a measure of sirop de cassis on top. Garnish with a slice of lemon and serve with straws.

GRECIAN

Blend together four parts peach juice, two parts orange juice, one part lemon juice and a scoop of crushed ice. Pour unstrained into the glass, add a squirt of soda water and garnish with fresh fruit.

(Above) Egg Nog, Capucine, Saint Clements, Queen Charlie, Lemonade Golden and (facing page) Nursery Fiz

JERSEY LILY

Stir a glass of fizzy apple juice with a little sugar, a dash of Angostura bitters and ice cubes. Strain and garnish with a maraschino cherry.

KEELPLATE

Shake together two parts tomato juice, on part clam juice, a couple of dashes of Worcestershire sauce and a good pinch of celery salt.

LEMONADE (FIZZY)

Pour the juice of a lemon into the glass an add two teaspoons of sugar. Stir until the sugar is dissolved, add four or five ice cub and top up with soda water. Garnish with slice of lemon.

LEMONADE (GOLDEN)

Shake together the juice of a lemon, a wine-glass of water, an egg yolk and two teaspoons of sugar. Strain into the glass, add ice cubes and garnish with fruit.

LEMONADE (PINK)

Make in the same way as still lemonade

(below) and stir in a tablespoon of sirop de framboise.

LEMONADE (STILL)

Shake together two scoops of crushed ice, the juice of a lemon and two teaspoons of sugar. Pour, unstrained, into the glass and top up with water. Garnish with a slice of lemon and serve with straws.

LEMON ICE CREAM SODA

Put two tablespoons of fresh lemon juice in a glass with two teaspoons of sugar and stir until the sugar is dissolved. Fill the glass two-thirds full with soda water and top with a large scoop of soft vanilla ice cream. Serve with straws and a spoon. Similarly, orange or grapefruit versions can be made.

LIMEADE

Shake together the juice of three limes and sugar to taste. Strain over ice cubes and add water or soda water. Garnish with fruit.

LIMEY

Shake together two parts lime juice, one part lemon juice and half an egg white. Garnish with a cherry.

MICKEY MOUSE

Over ice cubes pour cola, then add a scoop of soft vanilla ice cream, top with whipped cream and two cherries, and serve with straws and a spoon.

MOCK DAISY CRUSTA

Put two scoops of crushed ice into the glass and add the juice of two limes and a tablespoon of sirop de framboise. Top up with soda water and float a little grenadine on top. Garnish with a sprig of mint and raspberries on a stick.

NURSERY FIZZ

Over ice cubes pour equal parts orange juice and ginger ale. Garnish with a slice of orange and a cherry and serve with straws.

PRINCESS MARGARET

Blend together five or six strawberries, a slice of pineapple, the juice of half a lemon, juice of half an orange, a couple of dashes of sirop de fraise and a scoop of crushed ice. Pour into a sugar-frosted glass (stick the sugar with sirop de fraise rather than egg white or gomme), and garnish with a strawberry on the rim.

PUSSYFOOT

Shake together equal parts orange juice, lemon juice and lime juice, along with a dash of grenadine and an egg yolk. Add soda water if desired, garnish with a cherry and serve with straws.

QUEEN CHARLIE

Over ice cubes pour a measure of grenadine and top up with soda water. Garnish with a slice of lemon and a cherry on a stick, and serve with straws.

SAINT CLEMENTS

The name derives from the children's nursery rhyme "Oranges and lemons say the bells of Saint Clements..." and the drink is made by stirring equal parts of orange juice and bitter lemon with plenty of ice.

Serve garnished with slices of orange and lemon.

SAN FRANCISCO

Shake together equal parts orange juice, lemon juice, grapefruit juice and pineapple juice, along with an egg white and a dash of grenadine. Top up with soda water and garnish extravagantly!

SHIRLEY TEMPLE

Over ice cubes pour ginger ale and add a little grenadine. Stir and garnish with a cherry.

SOUTHERN BELLE

A non-alcoholic Mint Julep...Crush a sprig of mint with a teaspoon of sugar at the bottom of a glass, to extract the mint flavour. Add a squeeze of lemon juice and lots of ice. Top up with ginger ale, garnish with a sprig of mint and serve with straws.

SUMMERTIME SODA

Stir the juice of an orange with the juice of a lemon and the juice of a grapefruit. Pour over ice cubes and add soda water and a

Americano (above) and Acapulco Gold (facing page)

scoop of soft vanilla ice cream. Serve with straws and a spoon.

SURFER'S PARADISE

Over ice cubes pour the juice of half a lime and three dashes of Angostura bitters. Stir in lemonade to top up and garnish with a slice of orange.

TOMATO JUICE COCKTAIL

Shake together tomato juice, a good squeeze of lemon juice, a couple of dashes of Worcestershire sauce, a couple of drops of Tabasco, a pinch of celery salt and a shake of pepper. Strain and serve straight up or on the rocks. Garnish with a slice of lemon and a stick of celery.

YELLOW DWARF

Shake together one part orgeat syrup, one part cream and an egg yolk. Strain and add soda water to taste. Garnish with a maraschino cherry.

Prevention, as the saying goes, is better than cure…It is also less painful. A glass of milk and preferably a meal taken before you start drinking lines the stomach and protects against too harsh an onslaught. However, if you do wake up wishing you hadn't, knock back one of these monsters, and you may feel instantly revitalised. I do not necessarily guarantee their efficacy.

BULLSHOT

Shake together one part vodka, four parts condensed consommé or beef bouillon, a couple of dashes of Worcestershire sauce, a dash of lemon juice and a pinch of celery salt. Add Tabasco and pepper to taste.

CORPSE REVIVER COCKTAIL

Shake together one part brandy, four parts milk, a teaspoon of sugar or gomme syrup and a dash of Angostura bitters. Top up with soda water.

PICK-ME-UP

Stir one part cognac with one part pastis and one part dry vermouth.

PRAIRIE HEN

Into a small goblet pour a couple of dashes of vinegar and two teaspoons of Worcestershire sauce. Carefully break a

Prairie Oyst

whole egg into the glass without breaking the yolk, sprinkle with pepper and salt, and splash with a little Tabasco. Drink in one gulp.

PRAIRIE OYSTER

Into a small tumbler pour a teaspoon of Worcestershire sauce and a teaspoon of tomato sauce. Stir, and then gently add a whole, unbroken egg yolk. Splash with a little vinegar and dust with pepper. Drink one gulp.